Does Fish-God Know
Alan Summers

Yet To Be Named Free Press
Stoke-On-Trent, England
2012

Does Fish-God Know – Alan Summers

Collection copyright © 2012 Yet To Be Named Free Press. Individual poems copyright of Alan Summers and are used with permission. All rights reserved.

Yet To Be Named Free Press
www.yettobenamedfreepress.org

ISBN-13: 978-1479211043
ISBN-10: 1479211044

Dedicated to Karen.

My many thanks to the good people of haiku, my translator Hidenori Hiruta, and Emily Dickinson.

Pre

As this book is curiously lacking in cliché I feel I must add just one to emphasize the fact, so I'll keep the foreword short and let the poems speak for themselves.

If I must add a few words to justify a foreword, this book contains some of the strongest haiku written by Alan Summers, carefully chosen for their cerebral attack, backbone, humour and adaptive modelling. If you're familiar with Alan's work you'll be pleasantly surprised. If you're not familiar with his work then you'll be rushing out to buy other titles by him.

Alan Summers is one of Britain's top haiku writers, he ain't twee, nor is he brutal, he is somewhere in between, a place I like to occupy in coffee shops, police cells and waiting for trains . . . and my train window girls.

Brendan Slater, August 2012.

Does Fish-God Know

Alan Summers

Contents

Toy Suns, 11
Cupcake, 87
Shichi Fukujin, 155
General Publication Credits, 157
Award Credits, 158

Toy Suns

harvesting moon
the death of a friend's sister
a lost jigsaw piece

all those red apples amongst the blue tit

Does Fish-God Know

wild-eyed horses in Lichtenstein bubble gum wrappers

day moon
a first burn scar
off the oven tray

Does Fish-God Know

zeros and ones
Monsieur Verdoux
takes a bow

the sticky label
over the christmas card
the new boyfriend's name

Does Fish-God Know

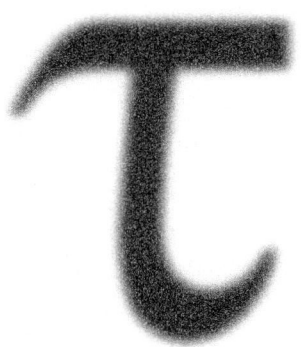

sultry evening
liquid from the take out bag
runs near the victim

Does Fish-God Know

Strawberry Hill
the mud off the vampire's
cloak

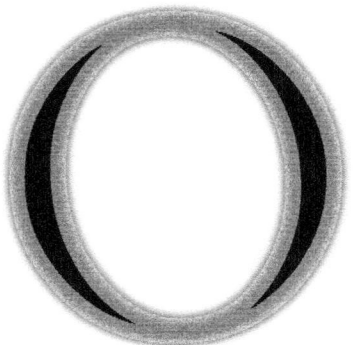

Does Fish-God Know

Mogao caves—
the hare with amber eyes
curls itself a timepiece

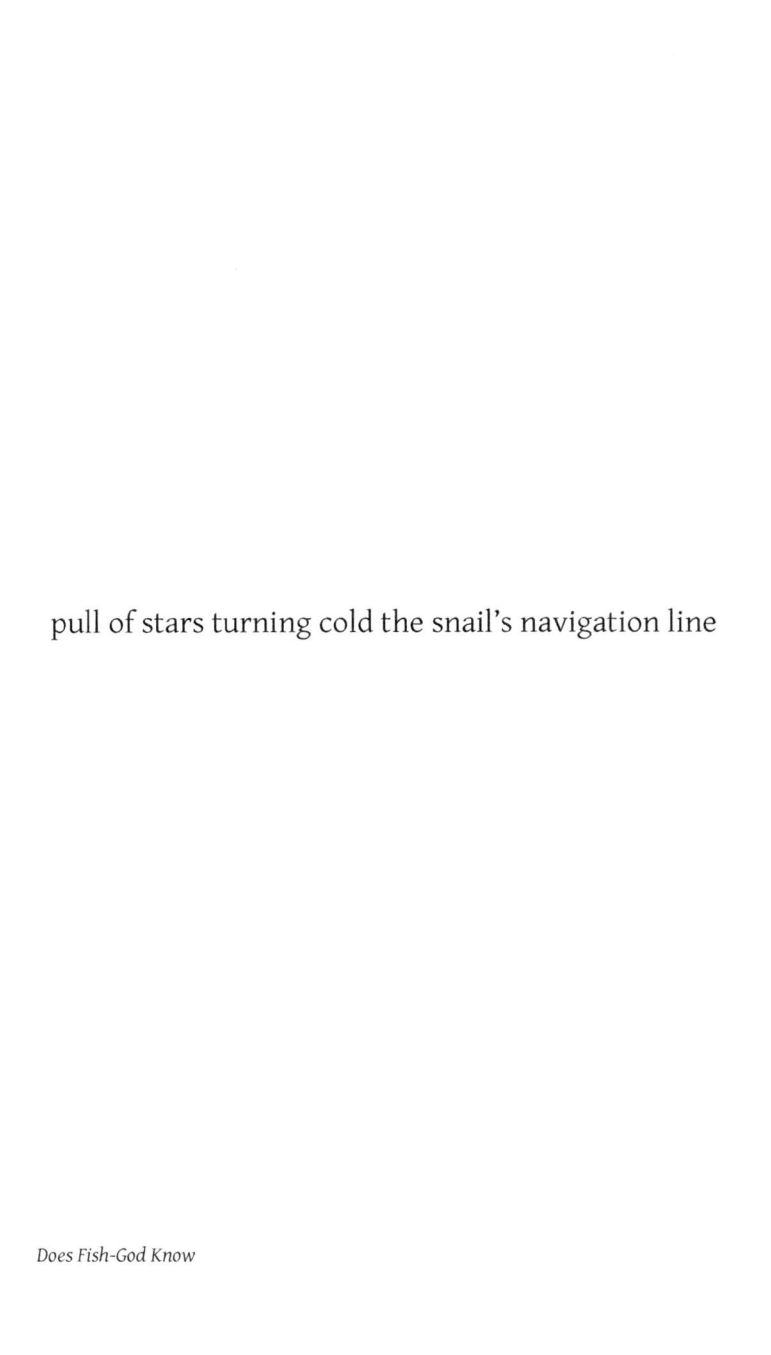

pull of stars turning cold the snail's navigation line

Does Fish-God Know

Sakurafubuki
you come to me

sunlit sweat
the young vagrant
sucks a thumb

Does Fish-God Know

the shadow
the shadow overtakes
is all his in this late hour

Does Fish-God Know

curse her Rain falls from a normal blue sky

crowded street
the space
a dog's deposit

Does Fish-God Know

Rethink
my clothes black
with crows

getting drunk
with the ripe moon
cadmium blues

Does Fish-God Know

toy suns
a winter-dark rain
smashes the city

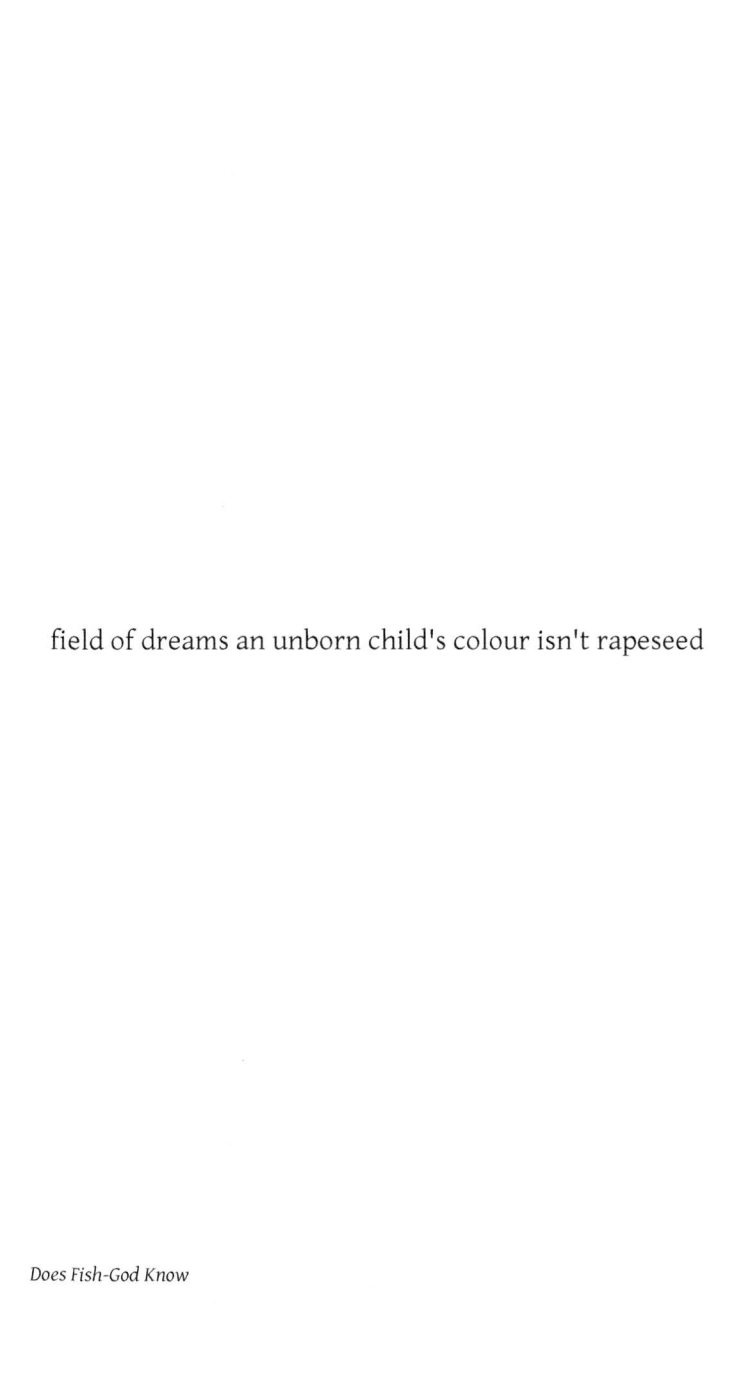

field of dreams an unborn child's colour isn't rapeseed

Does Fish-God Know

dreaming too long the garcinia man cuts deeply

scooter fall—
a boy grasps his pain
outside an art café

Does Fish-God Know

wind in the rain
if I could make a deal
with God

Does Fish-God Know

dirty secrets
my lifeline speckled
in leaf light

messenger shooting crows

Does Fish-God Know

cloud mountain
she screams her daughter's name
into the month of march

just me Great Auk I died

Does Fish-God Know

in the river reflection
he watches himself
watch the sunset

ghost knifefish
all the past lives flash
around me

Does Fish-God Know

petrichor this green sunsets in yesterday

a girl in a stone the big ask for clouds to be more bluer

Does Fish-God Know

aberrations of rain
epipubic bone retracts the lever

Pharmakós the name you scratch inside

Does Fish-God Know

end of matins
I decode into genomes
into petals

Ŭ

Does Fish-God Know

sleep disorder
the gas station lights
keep me company

cemetery entrance
clean anti-pigeon spikes
on the courtyard cross

Does Fish-God Know

midnight conversation
it's not always death
about lilies

dirty moon
last night
I trusted you

Does Fish-God Know

ń

snowfall she takes her daffodils Underground

Does Fish-God Know

train sitting:facingpeoplei'drathernot

Convolvulus
a word on my tongue
and the bumblebee

Does Fish-God Know

Monday's magician of yellow colour of murder

hot sandwiches
the railing spikes collect
children's gloves

Does Fish-God Know

this sorrowing heart fading into plum blossom

crowded train a dozen yellows crackle

Does Fish-God Know

this small ache
and all the rain
in the world

morning star
my train of thought
blocked by a train

Does Fish-God Know

don't trust the cat
her eyes green the earth
with anti-matter

place of fire
this part of the Novel
becomes my navel

Does Fish-God Know

ς

inner-city forest
a chameleon gives me
the undercover eye

Does Fish-God Know

Blood Moon
my Rhesus positive rising

bouncing rain
I force the hotel window
a little wider

Does Fish-God Know

macula lutea the snowballs inside dogs

my spare self
a vegetarian
on a meatship

Does Fish-God Know

vigilante movie
my elbow
heavy on your knee

sewer rat
breaking the water surface
its shut eye

Does Fish-God Know

Os Sacrum
this pear on Plato's diaphragm

does fish-god know?
rain can fall
from clear blue skies

Does Fish-God Know

bamboo in the rain
someone cutting deep
into my dream

vodka chilli cocktail
I become a corner
in the edge of a room

Does Fish-God Know

the grimace
of the roadside cat
its last

h=k=l=0 each love number sleeps

Does Fish-God Know

Van Gogh's wheatfield
a hand's-breadth of crows
stealing into my soul

gunsmoke tea
a dog argues
itself to death

Does Fish-God Know

street attack—
I hold the young girl
through her convulsions

morning moon
I think I met the man
who kills you

Does Fish-God Know

hot january
sweat drips
from a scalpel

Cupcake

sunday lunch
the chatter of children
among hard drinkers

Byztantine reasons
deep-water squid
feed the whale

Does Fish-God Know

Black Mountains
the stagnant chill
of snowmelt

zombie debt—
the practised slice
of a bread knife

Does Fish-God Know

Kafka's insect
. . . I share half-lives I didn't want

jazz opera
I learn all over again
my life is your life

Does Fish-God Know

rattle of rain
the crumbs in giants' pockets

Does Fish-God Know

the vagrant manoeuvre
a radio presses
to his head

different utopia
Quasimodo's private moon
over Notre Dame

Does Fish-God Know

Backscattered
from the lunar surface
the universe my shoe

cherry mist
the gun you pointed
as I said I love you

Does Fish-God Know

you ask me
what rhymes
with orange
deadheading

starlight just memory
the wink of a one-eyed dog
as it sneezes

Does Fish-God Know

Dizygotic
only the Small Things
are ever said

the mermaid's kiss
turning thirteen
i become a fish

Does Fish-God Know

4

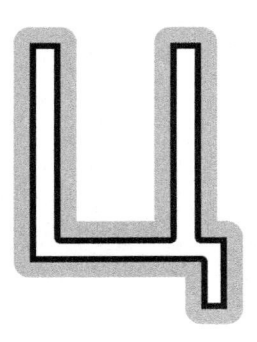

downtown
the window mist invades
my parking space

Does Fish-God Know

crazy moon
I wander lunarscapes
haiku by haiku

art café—
the security guy hums
a James Bond theme

Does Fish-God Know

fierce angel
I just want time to be
your cupcake

partial eclipse
the sky darkens then lightens
my cappuccino

Does Fish-God Know

kwĭkˈsĭlˌvər: I've a need for the next biblical cubit

b

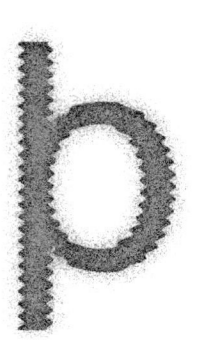

Does Fish-God Know

Sailor Moon
your first sērā fuku
saves the world

Old Curiosity Shop—
lacquered dolls
in the mid-day sun

Does Fish-God Know

overlooked crowbar—
all the stars are escaping
to light up offices

voodoo rain this new light year

Does Fish-God Know

bent
into his overcoat
the winter sky

sunnyside up
the autopsy shows
a decent breakfast

Does Fish-God Know

corn chaff realising oil as one colour

Does Fish-God Know

Plato's big picture
the meaningful differences
of infused foods

moonrise
I shine your chin of gold
and dimities of blue

Does Fish-God Know

unlacing the shoe
on his sole
mud from the gravesite

first quarter moon
dancing pinheads burst
into new angel DNA

Does Fish-God Know

dandelion wind
mending bridges
in the mist

lantana the dark-veined tiger nectar-laden

Does Fish-God Know

giallo this restricted area my birthplace

ā

Does Fish-God Know

reedmace & bluebells . . .
a torn porn magazine
off the cemetery path

Echo Beach
a plant wanderer
captures the sun

Does Fish-God Know

Red Sea beat my heart still hydrozoa

nitrating cellulose
and emulsion
new illnesses in the wind

Does Fish-God Know

powdered snow—
a crow's eyes above
the no parking sign

Does Fish-God Know

simplicity of night
the brittle cutting cold
of a moon sickle

Red Sea
stone fish penetrate
my rubber soul

Does Fish-God Know

beer forgotten
the drunk looks deep
within his shoe

cricket song
the jogger crunches
between loose gravel

Does Fish-God Know

Damien Hirst's butterflies disturbing the exhibits people

Eisenstein manoeuvre
a Flying Pope's
neutrality collides

Does Fish-God Know

tiredness
in the night train microcosm
yawns

hummingbird
I pull its colors
to create my own state

Does Fish-God Know

in the light
behind the toothpaste
one still cockroach

Emperor of Ice-Cream
my life as concupiscence
in a kitchen stanza

Does Fish-God Know

quantum bananas
the new church
of a keyboard wife

Does Fish-God Know

double thumbs
the supplicant's throat opens up
its tattoos

Sunheat—
also parted in death
a ladybird's wings

Does Fish-God Know

recurringdream#16.333iso/overbreakfast

beads of sweat
I lose myself in
the copulation of flies

Does Fish-God Know

Netsuke . . .
the hare with amber eyes
jumps back in again

Angel Beach
phytoplankton for the great whale

Does Fish-God Know

sick train the night heron shifts silt for all of us

Shichi Fukujin

on the makeshift map
we kiss
the lost cities

仮の地図今なき都市にキスをする

starlight cold
my finger traces the north star

星の光寒し
私の指は北極星をたどる

petal-like moon
over Fukushima
consoling people

花の月福島の民いやしけり

dealing with loss
my childhood in bookcovers

失いしものを取り上げる
本の表紙の中の私の子供時代

baby giggle
the man resurfaces
with sea-green eyes

赤ん坊がくすくす笑う
その人が再び姿を現す
海緑色の目をして

Myoken Bosatsu
your compass for safe voyage

妙見菩薩
航海安全のための羅針盤

EL verses © Alan Summers
Japanese trans. by Hidenori Hiruta

Does Fish-God Know

General publication credits

a handful of stones; Asahi Shimbun (Japan); Blithe Spirit; Beer Haiku Daily; Birmingham Words Magazine; #darkskies2010 *(a Twitter event supported by the Campaign to Protect Rural England in Shropshire)*; fox dreams ed. Aubrie Cox; haijinx; Haiku International (Japan); Haiku Friends Vol. 2 (Japan); Haiku Harvest: 2000 – 2006 (Modern English Tanka Press 2007); Haiku News; Haiku Spirit; Journal of Renga & Renku; Monostich; Notes from the Gean; paper wasp; Presence; Point Judith Light; Prune Juice journal of contemporary senryu, kyoka and haiga; Raku Teapot: Haiku (Raku Teapot Press/White Owl Publishing, California 2003); Raw NerVz; see haiku here (Japan); Snapshots (Snapshot Press); small stones anthology (2012); Shamrock, Haiku Journal of the Irish Haiku Society; Short Stuff ; still: a journal of short verse; Symmetry Pebbles; Temps Libre; The Bath Burp: Poetry, Music & Arts Monthly; THFhaiku app for iPhone/iPad/iPod Touch (2011); The Humours of Haiku (Iron Press 2012); The Mie Times (Japan); The Haiku Calendar, Snapshot Press (2004); Tinywords; The New Haiku, (Snapshot Press, 2002); The Haiku Foundation per diem (Monday 8/8/11); UKMO™ Collection; Watermark: A Poet's Notebook; World Haiku Review; NaHaiWriMo.

Award credits

does fish-god know?
Award credit: Winner of the Blithe Spirit Cover competition for issue 22/2 Autumn 2012 (for John Parsons cover artwork)

powdered snow
Award credit: Joint Winner, Haiku International Association (Japan) 10th Anniversary Haiku Contest 1999

beer forgotten
Award credit:
Runner up, Haiku Calendar Competition, Snapshot Press (2003)

sunday lunch
Award credit:
Editor's Choice, Haiku Harvest: 2000 – 2006 (Modern English Tanka Press 2007) (and magazine Haiku Harvest vol. 4 no. 1)

double thumbs
Award credit: 2nd Prize, Presence SciFaiku Contest (1998)

Netsuke ...
Award Credit: Honourable Mention, Best of Mainichi (Japan) 2011

bent
Award credit: Runner up, still magazine haiku competition (1998)

Printed in Great Britain
by Amazon